Rosa Mundi

THEO DORGAN
Rosa Mundi

SALMON  POETRY

Published in 1995 by
Salmon Publishing Ltd,
Upper Fairhill, Galway

A catalogue record for this book is available from the British Library.

ISBN 1 897648 64 2

Cover design by Theo Dorgan &
Poolbeg Group Services Ltd
Set in AGaramond 12/13
Printed by Colour Books,
Baldoyle Ind Est, Dublin 13.

Theo Dorgan was born in Cork in 1953. At present he works in Dublin as Director of Poetry Ireland/ Éigse Éireann, as a broadcaster with RTE Radio 1 and as an occasional journalist and reviewer.

Among his publications are *The Great Book of Ireland* (ed., with Gene Lambert, 1991), *Revising the Rising* (ed., with Máirín Ní Dhonnchadha, 1991), *The Ordinary House of Love* (1991, reprinted 1993) and *Kavanagh and After* (ed., 1995). Among his awards are The Listowel Prize for Poetry, 1992.

Acknowledgements

The author is grateful to the editors of the following publications in which these poems, or versions of them, first appeared:

The Irish Times, Poetry Ireland Review, Exposure, Windows, Cyphers, Undr, Poetry (Chicago), *Southern Plains Review* (USA), S*outhern Review* (USA), *Trinity Poetry Broadsheet, The Ripening of Time*

Some of these poems, or versions of them, have been broadcast on BBC Radio Ulster, BBC Radio 4, RTE Radio 1 and RTE Radio 2

"Nine Views of Uzbekhistan" first appeared as a pamphlet from The Harkin Press, Dublin 1992

"The Match Down the Park" was commissioned by Na Piarsaigh Hurling & Football Club, Cork, to mark their fiftieth anniversary

"To Gennadi Uranov in the Coming Times" won the Poetry Prize at Listowel Writers' Week, 1992

"The Geography of Armagh" was a runner-up in the British National Poetry Competition 1992

Thanks are due to Bernard and Mary Loughlin at The Tyrone Guthrie Centre, Annaghmakerrig, and to the following people: Paula Meehan, Tony Curtis, Pat Boran, James McAuley, Philip Casey and Gregory O'Donoghue.

for
Paula Meehan

Even as we freeze in Lethe
we will remember
the seven heavens
this earth cost us.

— Osip Mandelstam

Contents

prologue

name on stone
shadow on path
moon behind
latticework of branches
all so deceptively simple
the wind over the crosses
the name on the wind

I had that name
and lived between those dates
printed on paper, carved in stone —
I was the seed and now am clay
this birch more part of me than you are

Thornship

A thornship lifted from the blown hedge,
White rags to carry her head
And a wren her pilot.

High in the blue of March a hawk wheeled
Out of the archaic, and a crow's rattle
Cawed out along her wake.

I set my heart to follow her lift,
Shifting my ground as to the manner born —
Borne up and out with her,

The spume of blossom dusting my eyes.
The wind thrummed in her rigging,
The wren dropped back

Along her broad track and she dipped for the north,
A fine strain in her ribs, her decking
Meticulously fit.

How long she rose and where she carried us,
What we saw from that height, how many
We were, and from where,

Doesn't matter now. Dream up alongside,
My salty love of May, settle your feathers
Here beside me, fit for the journey.

House over the Harbour at Ballintoy

for Joan and Kate Newmann

Carrick-a-Rede, Port Ballintrae, the Causeway,
A long day spun out in sea and granite. We turn
On a whim into a tight-wound hill and down past
An alien house to Ballintoy —

Not a room in that house where a man or
woman could
Stretch out, built by an artist to face down the
        nights:
The view is west to Donegal and the basalt columns
Of a fallen city.

Chamber-tombs, passage-graves and double raths,
        Union
Flags and bunting to confuse the French visitor.
Our friends pick flint and herb from the day's flow
To season their lives.

A disjointed land.

We play at tourists, unhappy and at home
Where the road from Tara ends in Dunseverick
        crumbling
On its rock, and a snug harbour opens
New arms to Scotland.

The eye picks trim pleasure-boats at anchor,
        children galvanic
Where waves foam through a notch in rocks;
        Greeks would
Have tavernas here, lamb from the hill fields
        smoking

On charcoal with Atlantic fish,

But, the times that are in it, the fresh quay walls,
    the landing stage
Tempt a military read: a perfect harbour for landing
    craft, enough
Room to turn a truck. A discreet place to work into
    if the worst
Should come to the worst.

I've read that the Swiss build highways with air
    force jets in mind,
As Haussmann laid out the boulevards for their
    lines of fire —
What a species we are for value, the savings
    recouped in
Overlapping maps.

As I roved out,

Indeed. I reach my hand up to my love walking the
    wall,
Pure happy. I imagine pushing her face into gravel
    as the shots ring out,
Cowering as heavy boots smack desperately for
    cover, or the heart-
Stopping silence as

Dressing behind rocks we hear the van's engine, the
muffled outboard
In the darkened bay. I think of the architect Albert
    Speer. The strange house
Is a watchtower for times of shallow sleep, when
    boats at night
Make the skin crawl like the sea.

Train to Derry

A crow beats on the updraft over a high hawthorn,
Rocked, but plunging on. A stick of Paras, bristling
    with nerves,
Coughs and boots forward along the sheugh.
Long after the soldiers have gone, the crows will
    settle home.

Since Newry, choppers have been battling back and
    forth
Across the track. These trains are overheated, sweat
Stings in my underslept eyes, I'd rather the crows'
    lift and pluck
Than to be here, rocked to the quick, driving on
    Derry.

I often wish, my love, that we were birds, the wide
    domains
Of Ireland at our turn and fall, the world's wind
Our natural element — rain, ice, hail or sun our
    gods,
The tall pines our greenwhip lightning rods.

∞

Tonight there's a horned moon and Venus trailing
Low over the Waterside. Tonight let me fold you in
    my wings,
Pray nobody's killed in dark of country or town.
    We'll settle
The long night in another of our beds, watch what
    the morning brings.

November in May

Trees in their full weight buffeted by rain,
The plants on the windowsill waterlogged,
A gale pushing down the canyons of garden
Between two tall rows of Georgian houses.

Aerials whip in the wind, birds battered low
Go by in fits and starts, the elderflowers are dull
In the sulphurous light, night coming over us
Too early, far too early. We stand at the window

Cradling cups of tea, trying not to feel cheated.
It was a long winter, God knows, there were days
We hardly thought to survive, and now this wind
Battering the glass is breaking our hearts.

Listen, can you hear them breaking? Small sounds,
Skitter of claws on slate, mortar tumbling
To a flat roof. A siren grumbles along the canal,
      muted
And shredded under the weight of the rocking gale.

And still the night to get through, a night of rain
      falling
While we seek refuge in books, in small, careful
      sentences
And guarded looks. We walk from room to room
      avoiding
The bed, talk of the future, the glare of the
      calendar.

The Geography of Armagh

Somebody's lover is leaving someone home,
A neighbourly duty, a mile or two down
A winding country road.

The orchards are heavy with fruit and dust,
The road unrolling into autumn,
A winding country road.

Somebody's lover at the end of the command wire
Watches the headlights burrowing down
A winding country road,

Tense as the front wheels bite on a bend
And the car straddles the culvert, then
A winding country road

Blown slow, skyward into the harvest moon,
Apples hung in the flame tree,
A winding country road

Whipcracking aftershock, fountain of earth and
       fire,
And then the meat and apples settling,
A winding country road

Strewn with glass, branch, leaf, flesh, somebody's
       lover
And his neighbour — the what's left — and
A winding country road

Going God alone knows where, a root-flamed ash,
A wire snapped, as somebody's lover takes to
A winding country road.

Somewhere

Somewhere there is a simple life,
The snow dredged through a stand of birch,
Tracks of a rabbit in the snow, the path
Indented on the white page; track
Of the wood-cutter, the solitary doctor, the child
Trailing homeward to soup, firelight, mother.

I hold this vision in my cupped hands,
A dome of light on the bare table;
There was anguish in that ornament, the shaken
      snow
Made the plastic cottage frail —
I almost remembered a trail home, sitting at home
In firelight, tasting the soup of another life.

Mother, I have been in the cold places I dreamed of
When you were proud of your bright son.
The day the bus went by the back road to
      Sheremetyevo
I snatched beriozka from the rattle of pale trunks,
The word echoing. Tracks of a rabbit in the snow,
My own tracks crossing the trail of childhood.

Never again, my mother, those conversations
      by firelight.
Somewhere, somewhere there is a simple life.

Red Square

Crack of red silk in the arctic uplights,
Yellow of Leningrad in the walls and domes,
Oxblood-dull the crenellated walls.

Cresting the rise before the cobbled square,
Stone of St. Basil's freighted with bright turbans.
I imagine tank tracks crunching across the setts,

I imagine the steppe wind howling from immense
Voids far to the east, but this is a dull night
Of afterheat and haze. The square is tired.

It has seen too much of history, too many couples
From solemn places with wedding garlands
For Lenin's tomb, old women burdened

With perhaps-bags, waiting for wind of change,
For a flash of lost gaiety, a surprising question.
The stage is set for a new brute and his programme.

Of Certain Architects, Technicians and Butchers

I am the belly of great armies
I battle the ages in my fear
I am the horror in the newborn child
And the horror in its mother.
Who but I built Ulm cathedral?

I am the great cathedrals of pure thought
I am the frozen wave of the Carpathians
I am the sword that cleaves the knot forever
And the knot itself that closes around the sword.
Who but myself made Alexander weep?

I am the famine when Alexanders weep
I am the sand that built and swallowed Carthage
I am the Hydra drinking Stalin's blood
And the blood that doused the flames of Dresden.
Who but I could darken the air with engines?

I am the engines and the fire at heart
I am the garden and gardener at Treblinka
I am the wolf who howls in Katyn Forest
And the forest itself howling in the wolf.
Who but I would storm the moon?

    I am a forest of great armies
    I am the knot that twists the child
    I am the sword turns in engines
    I am the wolf in the cathedral.

I pace behind mountains, turning the days over,
I wait for the dark star that will shine when I cross.

Nine Views of Uzbekhistan

Roses in a bank of snow
Birds of paradise,
Leaves in a spring tree —
The eyes of an Uzbekh dancing girl.

But wasn't there a curfew?
A flight of masked glances,
A downturning of palms.
A journalistic error, it happens.

Salaam aleikum, not *zdrastvuitye*.
Rachmat, not *spassiba bolshoi*.
This thaws even apparatchiks,
The Union sailing over a reef of vowels.

A police escort fore and aft,
Traffic halted at all the junctions.
It is meant for courtesy but, being Irish,
We exchange sceptical glances.

Nasruddin teaching his donkey to read,
Nasruddin as an Asian Sancho Panza —
Twenty five centuries since Alexander ruled
This people whose heroes are tyrants and jokers.

Timurlane's teacher has the bigger
tomb
But Timurlane's is the name we know;
Statues of Lenin everywhere we go,
Here and there Nasruddin and his donkey.

Pomegranates, melons, dust and straw
In a market old before Christ was born.
A schoolboy with Ulugbek's eyes greets us
In French. He says he is pleased to see us.

> He might be my father's father, he sits on
> A spavined donkey as if he might ride to
>   Vienna.
> Where from? The eyes unwinking. Ah, Ireland.
> Green island. Beyond England, farther than
>   Moscow.

The exquisite mosque has been a museum
Since the Revolution, open to all. Last year
The Mullahs paraded, demanding reconsecration.
Ah Jaysus, says one of the lads, I hope you said no.

Béal na mBláth

I have been so long waiting
To say what I must say
The voice of flowers has left me.

Winter is always here.
Stone and water mix in my breath,
A voice divided against itself.

To Gennadi Uranov in the Coming Times

The birches are cooling after a sultry day, and grass
Is springing back in the wind of evening. The paths
Are dusty, the sound from behind the railings
Is the chatter of starlings before dark.

There is the feeling of early in the century, a face at
One of these high windows might have echoed
In Anna Andreevna's heart, pale signal
Of love lost, of smoky music, the melancholy heart.

She dreamed of a simple life, as our poet dreamed
Whose house soaks in the fading light of day;
He turned his face against the century's wall, and
    she
Walked humbly into the future of her art.

This man had set his heart on passion's play,
Ended in rage that the hero's day was done.
This woman, born to aristocratic ways,
Turned to her destiny in a prison's dark.

Walking tonight, I turn their verses over,
Sounding the voices of our time,
Trying the shape ahead of me in this park
Of what is terrible in the days to come.

My heart is muffled like a mourning drum.
There has been so much mourning, wave after wave
Climbing the wall of the century, smashing
Our courage to splinters of stars

And this is all we have to carry forward:
Starlight of prisons, flints & shards of all that is best

In us, a line here, a phrase there, our honour
And glory in fragments over the wide earth.

Tonight I will walk down to the dark Liffey
And stand there until I cannot feel the cold
    anymore.
I will think of you on the Moskva's embankment
Remembering this city, fearing for your own,

And though I am a melancholy pagan
I will pray for an end to this terrible century,
For quiet in your house and in mine, silence
After music for Yeats and Akhmatova.

Garda Waking from a Dream of Language

The rock and tilt of it, the red-wrapped
Rump and pelvis of a whore against
The slow beat of my own country feet.
In the railed Square, earth and green
Breathing to the right of me, asphalt
To the left, and over it all the unknowing
Clouds and above the clouds the loanwords
Of stars, jet-trails, hard constellations.

I think of the lies I will be told now if I stop
The young girl with cider in her basket, space
Behind her eyes, or the cyclist impatient and
        testy —
There is no rain, and little traffic, the frame is
Light, he's nimble, why should he carry a lamp?
Everyone reaches first for the greasy words,
Evasive, investing what's plain with fog and doubt.

The squawk-box on my shoulder at least is
Plain, it spits digits, location of units, codes
For crimes and seriousness, names — the slick
Electric tracking of the game. Tonight I could trace
Answers to questions, right from the foaming
        nations
Who had the first grace of cities to this shop-
Window that gives me back my uniform, behind
        bars.

I think we learned language first beneath plain stars.
Maybe a Persian watchman, or a Greek
Walking the unquiet nights like this was first
To speak plain against night's unease, the rock
And tilt of it questioned by the red-wrapped

Rump and pelvis of a whore, who writes
Need and independence into the balance of the
        night,
Who answers me plain and simple from her door.

Speak plain,they told me, say what you mean and
Mean what you say. Then it must follow as the
        night.
The day. Such confidence, father and mother, in
        your truth.
How would you name these currents, crossed and
        backed?
All night the roar of holiday jets, lick of quick
        traffic,
Background the chaos logged with such precision in
My ear. Sometimes I ask myself what I'm doing
        here.
For answer incline and listen to my feet, resume the
        beat.

Would I be better, as you dreamed for me,
Easing the car now through a soft country lane,
        home
From a dance with perfume on my hands, thinking
That one, now, is nice, she'd do me grand. Arcadian
Dreams to shepherd a language home? There's
A queer word, one that'd lose a sergeant. I choose,
And they won't understand me, in spite of all,
The script of street and city, this hard full stop.

Kilmainham Gaol, Dublin,
Easter 1991

for Frank Harte

Roadies in ponytails stringing lights and cables,
A beer can popped in the corner, echo of sound
    check.
Outside in the filling yard, hum of expectation.

We pour through the narrow gate under the gallows
    hook
In twos and threes, becoming an audience.
Before the lights go down we examine each other
    shyly.

The singer surveys his audience, heat rising
To the tricolour and plough overhead.
As the first words of Galvin's lament climb to
    invoke
James Connolly's ghost, we are joined by the dead.

∞

I say this as calmly as I can. The gaunt dead
Crowded the catwalks, shirtsleeved, disbelieving.
The guards had long since vanished, but these
Looked down on us, their faces pale.

I saw men there who had never made their peace,
Men who had failed these many years to accept
    their fate,
Still stunned by gunfire, wounds, fear for their
    families;
Paralysed until now by the long volleys of May so
    long ago.

I think that we all felt it, their doubt and their new
    fear,
The emblems so familiar, the setting, our upturned
    faces,
So unreal. Only the dignity of the singer's art
Had power to release them. I felt it, I say this
    calmly.

I saw them leave, in twos and threes, as the song
    ended.
I do not know that there is a heaven but I saw their
    souls
Fan upward like leaves from a dry book, sped out
    into the night
By volleys of applause; sped out, I hope, into some
    light at last.

I do not know that I will ever be the same again.
That soft-footed gathering of the dead into their
    peace
Was like something out of a book. In Kilmainham
    Gaol
 I saw this, I felt this. I say this as calmly and
    lovingly as I can.

Seven Versions of Loss Eternal

1

Imagine the salt caking an evening sand-rose,
A steep dune sprawling towards the infinite,
A lone traveller trying hard not to fall
Lost in the sands of love and fought-for trinities —
Imagine his thirst for reconciling fountains,
For the three jets made one in the sun's blind
    strobe,
For the three paths rounding to where she waits.

2

Green cracked linoleum, the oak door shredding
Wind and rain-dark into spindrift,
Dust and hot paint behind him, the day's labour
Already lost in a settling of files. Hand on his collar
He pauses a moment, irresolute, almost lost
But she is not there, never will be again. A paper
    clip
Clicks against change in his pocket, and here's his
    bus.

3

What it must be like from space, imagine,
The child's nightmare downwardness, the globe
Blue, green and watered, the great mountains
Scored like ribs across a carcase, cities
Winking on and off, deltas a great scrawl
Of mud and silt on the blue-green flush of silk —
To be there, and never to go down again.

4

The projector ticks as it cools, metal and glass
Going lifeless with electricity shut off. His hand
Spins with the deadweight of the rewind arms,
His mind as vacant as the cinema far below.
In the tang of hot celluloid he hesitates to think
Of where he might go now there is nowhere to go,
A man becoming a shadow of himself.

5

Imagine the great Atlantic waves, rearing to freeze
Far over him — embattled and stubborn, raw from
        spray
And cold and drenching, the radio gone, the stars
unseen
For days now, unable for even a moment to go
        below;
A rag of topsail's enough to drive him on, harder
        and deeper
By the minute, as long as his wrists hold out.
Her blue handkerchief wound around his
watchstrap.

6

Salt on the butcher block of beech, he leanshard
On his circling hands, the brush scouring the work
        away
In the blue light from the window. He has learned
Not to breathe too deeply in this quiet time, never
To look at his hands until he has scrubbed
them clean.

He clicks off the light with his back to the
        street,
The most terrifying moment of his day.

7

Imagine your whole day is a search for a missing
        sign —
You scan rivers of paper, faces drifted in the streets,
Magazine illustrations, cinema posters, the blank
Windows of schools, offices, factories. You listen
To bus tyres in the rain, at night you sneak sudden
        glances
At clouds ripping past the stars. Nothing.
An irregular contraction in the chest. Nothing.

A Neighbour of Ours

for Gerry Murphy

The lift of a linnet's wing was all he asked,
With the fog a light gold over the brewery and
The bells tumbling over sweet Blackpool
From the North Chapel, Shandon, the Assumption,
To be standing on Richmond Hill
And the pale sun shining,
A day in October, the air clear in his head.

Nothing out of the ordinary, a simple perfect
     moment,
The lift of a linnet's wing was all he asked for
     and got.

The Life I Live Now

I throw my head back in the street,
In the hum of evening traffic
On the black and rainslick street.
I regard the stars without feeling.

As if they were raindrops in a web,

As if they were phrases in an electric
Frame, crystals that might arc into
My skull like perfect diminutives —
To die in my heart, where you have died.

A Man is Standing on a White Beach, Knowing that He Must Die

It rolls on the crisp white shore,
Folds in upon itself and comes to rest
Back in the darkness from the lamplight pool,
All I ever cared for in this life.

It might be a poem, the language salt with life,
Teasing the memory of Sunday by a pool,
Or it might be your words, first laboured, then at
    rest,
Recalled while we watch this unfamiliar shore.

Nothing is ever simple on this shore —
Here where the page is margin to a life —
No more than light that gathers in a pool
Hungry to taste a sea that cannot rest.

Whatever, I know I never will have rest
Until the isolated moments pool
And we stand out to speak of simple life,
The dead words abandoned on the shore.

What Lives We Lead

I woke from dreams of gunfire to the sound of
    sirens,
Crossing my own footsteps at a remove in time.

Without leaving my bed, suddenly I was there.

So many ambush points in a known place,
The precise angle where two walls meet,
The exact shadow cast by a hanging sign.
He was there in the plane of light from the great
    window,
My younger self, that dust-devil,
Turning forever angrily on himself.

Brewery men dropping barrels onto a stuffed sack,
The dull percussive thuds, the cheerful obscenities
And the half-humorous eyes, angling from under
    caps —
I must have looked odd, stopping suddenly as if
    struck.

So many years ago, and the pain again so piercing.
What lives we lead, after all!

Trial by Existence

I am the bright, electric child
Flattened against the fading blue of night,
I am the child of love made in the dark
By bodies urgent to touch what does not die.

I am the ghostchild of the timelines
In the air outside your window,
Riding the updraft like a leaf
I am as blue and bright as sudden grief.

With your companion you carve the hidden light,
Each gesture, each caress breaking the husk and
Tuning the worldlines to a pulsing mesh until
Bodies break from flesh, until there is breath only,
Climbing to fuse in breath, and light
Stabs in the dark like a runway beacon.

I am the child of light from far-off stars,
Sucked from a clean run through space
Down through the whirlpool of raw need,
The cry of the womb for fulness, a charm against
    death.

I am the spark to leap the gap, I am the gap that I
    must cross.
When the air is thick with passion I lean on your
    lungs,
When you burn and reach out it is I who burn,
It is towards me that you forever reach.

I am the child eager for life, listen to me,
I am a bitter death where love is not.
I am a star in daytime and good health
Where the room rocks in the pitch of hard-won
love.

The Inquisitor Considers the Daughters of Eve

Before they are born I love their unmoving silence,
But when the rot sets in and breath draws life
From silence and their eyes open, it all starts up —
The long webs of arrogance and decay.

Their flesh is enchanted by a word,
Womanjuice, corruption, seed and clay
Reduced in a sweaty sac. Choice is their word
For what they lack, chosen obedience to the will of
	God.

Death is my enemy and choice is death's word.
When I hear it whispered in my ear at night I know
The Devil walks, and wake to sweat and pray —
We were not made to choose but to obey.

They spin and dip like insects over the festering
	earth,
Liars and witches who would burn for shame
If they heard God's word on them, if they knew the
Word
As I do, who am sent among them with a sword of
	fire.

All day in the city there is murmuring against me.
The women say I corrupt the young, they say my
	photographs
And specimens are evil, they say their children lie
	awake
Rigid with fear because of me, because of my
	witness.

Let their children gag on truth: the only beauty is
    unborn.
There is no innocence in the quick, let them burn
In their beds, let them do the Will from fear
If from nothing else. My father taught me there is
    nothing else.

I Remember a Night in the Long Valley

There we were with the light
Pouring out of us onto
The round and famous table.
Even Humphrey was laughing,

Calling Time! Time!
Like a barman in a fable.
In the wind off the clock
The red-eyed drinkers turned

Half-faces towards us:
The fang and the smile,
Benediction and curse.
The bells boomed

In my head, the familiar
Sliding slow into the strange.
Somebody kissed my ear.
The spittle after — sticky, cold.

The Woman who was an Eagle

She is a voice through which stone extends an
     empire.
She is a silence deeper than my most vertiginous fall
Into fear. She'd stop me now with one swift look.
     Her
Dreaming is redolent of the sea at nightfall, pulsing
     salt.

When she'd come from the garden, green would
     come with her.
I have seen her at dusk become luminous in an
     owl's call
Of salutation. Beads burn in the stream of her
     speech. Where
She'd walk I would range behind her, scarcely
     daring talk.

Mountain, moorland, where I am blind she sees
     entire.
Lands I tremble at she has claimed, traversed,
     survived. And all
Enriches her. She has never looked for comfort. Her
     heart
Is a well, sunk in rich earth and rock, down which I
     fall.

She has placed on my tongue salt of forgetting, I
     will not forget.
I bite back my voice in the city streets, finding no
     place to speak her name.

She Says

Empty yourself,
Red wine wells to the lip

It is time now,
And already too late

Forget me,
I am always with you.

Drowned in wine and forgetfulness
Breathe easy, loose your grip,

I call all things to dance with me
In the ripening of time.

A Slow Poem

I place my finger with great care
On the sleeping magnificent body of my beloved.
The room is quiet and huge, the air still, so still
I hear dustmotes falling like leaves on the
    counterpane.

I stop my breathing and she fills me up
With swell of breath, the rise and fall of tides
So quiet and silver there, I am carried up and out of
    touch;

And she is far below, curled into me,
Her skin sufficient boundary, her dreams and
    trouble stilled.
Her troubles become diamond in my chest, I tip
    and balance

Here beneath the ceiling, full of airy, thoughtful
    love, then fall
As slowly as leaves falling on a field,
Until I settle there beside her, breathing her breath.

The Backward Look

Summer was standing in the high corn, the stems
Stiff with minerals, the seed-husks packed with
    bread.

You breasted feathered heads, wading towards me,
    your eyes
Blazing, your palms like rudders trailing and a swift

Dropped suddenly out of the blue, tracing a perfect
    arc,
A flash of compact muscle bursting past.

And still you came on, and still I see you wading,
Your brown bare feet scuffing the dust,

With each pace nearer as the picture recedes and
    you are framed
By the long hill that rises up behind you

In willowherb, heather, gorse and ash. Draw close,
    the fire
Is glowing in the hearth, nest your dark head here
    on my shoulder

And see what I see: high summer, the life that is to
    be,
Me like a scarecrow planted there, heart packed

With straw and joy and promise, a swift
stitching the compact
That brings you on. Rain beats on the
    window, a gust

Rattles the chimney-pots but the fire's well
set, and bread
Is cooling in the kitchen. Our kitchen. Our first
summer. This life.

The Second Fortune

Between what is and what is not
We walked, the Huntress loosed a shot.

Before and after, we were there —
The arrow pierced but singing air.

That, my love, was quite an art,
To be together and apart

Yet we, transparent, without fear —
What were we but singing air?

On Knockmealdown

And, you ask, is there a song
Naming this land laid low beneath?

Only this turbulent wind, driving from
Here down through the oceanic trees.

The Edge

In a million mites of crystal
The beach dreams fusing to glass.

The high sun yearns for the blue
Forgetfulness of the blue sea.

Miro's House for Lovers

My love, he writes, I have found us a house,
A farmhouse in Catalonia, such a house
As would shelter dreaming lovers.

There is a tree in the garden, rooted
In the void, shod in white enamel against goats.
It has leaves like the feathers of wet crows.

The ground floor was a stable once,
The top floor a granary. The windows are small,
Neat against wind and sun.

There is a lean-to with an old hooped wagon,
A cistern for drawing water, a columbarium,
And oh, the red, red earth of the garden!

Listen to me, the light is exactly right.
The letter of all beginnings could root in that light
Under a sky so blue the midday moon shines
        through.

A Charm on the Night of Your Birthday

I light the sky above our bed for you
With seven stars of gold, ploughing
The deeps for you — and that's not so hard
When you are the sea.

I rock in my ribs here in your absence,
My heart like a diesel thudding away
And you at the helm, friend and guide
Steering through for me.

I'll sleep now, soon, under seven stars,
The plough in the night dipping towards you,
Your ghost on deck above holding our course,
Your bones asleep in me.

My blue pillow is wrapped in your shirt
And my head is bedded in the scent of your hair,
I'll make your hair a sail to carry me
From here to over there.

Western

A painted pony floats in tall grass
Rises and plunges with
All the time in the world.

The grasses are dryheaded, flecky with dust
They wheel out around him in great arcs
Under billows of wind.

The day's weight goes down in his plunge,
The air heaves with his roll of shoulder.
Telescope in on his seedflecked hock, his unwinking
    eye.

The bridle is plaited rope. A wishbone of sweat
On back and flanks where the rider was.
She is floating now through the tall grass

The lark and the swift see her bent back
And the cracked stalk milks her step and instep.
The wind dips, tips my scent into her face.

She holds the hunting-blade low in her fist,
The grasses brush at her breasts and belly,
Her hunter's cheekbone, striped with desire.

A red sun glares from the Dublin mountains,
I slip into a downdraft, dropping east from the
    ridge.

The Odds

Fan of black hair against the pillow
We have been here before

What light there is
Gathers into her star pupils.

She is thinking of sandwaves
Drifted against sunset,
And he is thinking of rain
Scudding through grasses
Against the wall of her house.

Night beats on the window.
Will it be this time?
Neither can tell.
For now there is sand
Against rain, chance
Against destiny.

The nerve of risk
Flicking against adultery.

Enchanted, she murmurs,
Testing the word on his face,
I am *enchanted.*

The Astronomer of Love

Out there, a galaxy
Curls in upon itself,
Hung
In the sparkling bowl of night —

I am testing this when
Between breath and breath
I flick sideways
And find you fragile in your flight.

Light in the cheekbones
Breaking through,
Light in the sockets
Beneath clamped lids,

A bronze warrior
Fit for
The shock of steel on bone,
But plunging on

Into the heart of night,
Ice plumes fanning wide
Into the wake of your wild rise

Far from the home planet,
Aimed at the world out there,
The ice becoming silver
In your hair.

Between breath and breath I brush
A kiss upon your cheek.
You open direct from sleep,
A nebula whirling in each fabulous eye.

Me, John Wayne &
the Delights of Lust

Sometimes I wake and find you
So trustingly curled against me
I forget to breathe.
The impulse toward sentiment
Irresistible, I back away down the ladder
With that aw-shucks John Wayne face on
And go to make tea,
Counting my blessings as diligently
As the child I was would tell his rosaries
Before he got sense.

I get sense, returning with the heavy tray,
When you stir, crack an eye open and say
"Oh love, what kind of morning is it . . ."
Nothing in this new world better than
That moment when, me laid up alongside
And the waves ebbing towards the planted palm
By the window, you stretch to your full length
And light two cigarettes, fixing me with a grin
And an out-of-focus, complicit, quizzical look.
John Wayne to hell, I think, and phone in sick.

Driver

for M.B.

Rain beats on the windshield as she drives,
Rain of the southern winter under the Cross.
Rain slicks from the tyres as she takes curves,
One after the other, in slow motion.

The white line unpeels before her eyes,
An envelope thumbed open, the letter
     showing through.
She leans into the next curve, and the next,
Impatient to read the signature, to read . . . *love*,

The rain is everywhere tonight, even
The radio plays Rainy Night in Georgia,
It is like that when you are caught, the world
Rounding to a closed set of curves.

Absolute concentration empties her out
Into the night, her hands on the wheel
Are light but firm, as if gripping his shoulders
— which slowly, imperceptibly, she is.

A letter is waiting for her at journey's end,
She smiles, shifting down to third,
Smiles and sobers to think what lies behind cliché,
Hearing what beats on the windshield as his voice.

Something hypnotic in the long procession of
     curves,
The low hum of tyre-grooves in light rain,
Sets her to settle back easy in her heart,
To wind the whole journey into a song of his name.

Under Mercury

My blood and my brain are bound to his rule,
That trickster and lightfoot, the male thief
Who watched over my birth.

Sometimes a solid earthflush fills my veins,
As now, watching your feet flick out,
Inviting the plunge.
And I think that I could live like this
But it never quite works out.

Sooner or later we both come and then it's
Me for the gate of disappearances,
The blue silence, love's long dark.

Valley Dream

There is a valley crested with broad pine,
Threaded with rivers and willow, opening
Westward to the sea. I saw us there last night
On a low ridge, as the sun was going down.

Martin, swift or swallow, it wasn't clear
What the birds were, flickering on the staves
The powerlines made stepping out across the valley.
They stitched and unpicked the twilight,
  a song of air.

You sighed, and my breathing settled; stretched,
And a great ease flowed through my limbs.
You turned, and splinters of late sunlight
Glanced from your eyes, cut razor-sharp through
  mine.

She Buckles in Her Sleep

Close now, the hurt that has you hurt yourself.

I hear it trickle over the cut edge in your sleep,
The drain of meaning, trust, all that we have
To sing back the dark, the spirit's poverty.

Curl in my arms and sigh, and settle here.
I am no saint or saviour, and I am your grief
Too often, though I would not be.

Shelter, shelter and kindness, this embrace
And this belief: we are nearing the still centre
Where love is again possible, and strange, and rich.

White Stone Promises

If on a dark night after searching
Until my mind is nearly gone from me
I bring you your mother Akhmatova
With her pale hands turned young again
To soothe the unquiet from your face,
What will you do for me?

I ask three things only:

A night and a day in the dark
Of your eyes without sleep,

The stone that Fearbhlaidh had from Cearbhall
With the white of your breast in it,

Never to leave my dreaming
Without saying where you may be found.

Crossing the Shannon in broad sunlight
I ask these things of you.
You shall have what you need
While there is breath in me.

First Lesson

Space within and space without
I made a body with a shout.
You flowed around me into trees
And soothed me with song.

Sun within and sun without,
Revolving I called up a drought.
My dry breath scorched the trees,
You fled into a thread of water.

Space within and sun without,
I blessed the world with a strong shout.
A green breeze revived the trees
And you came back to flow inside me.

Cryptic tales are quickly told
And hold the mind has wit to hold them.
Only experts of the heart
Will understand your gift, my art.

Her Hawk, Her Messenger

This also, to be
Spreadeagled on a tossed bed
Scream of hawk in the high pines
Resin on the air, unmerciful light
On the whitewash wall
Noon, not her hour
So where does this come from
Again and again
The crescent axeblade sighing through skin
The bone spraying out in white chips
Blood spraying out after bone
Through the ribs over and over
The same blow forever and ever
Again and again
Spreadeagled on a tossed bed
My head on your dress
Lead in ankle and wrist
A starfish on the ironframe bed
Again and again
Resin on the air, and blood
Scream of a hawk
The axe from behind through the ribs
Over the heart
And the heart feeling nothing, nothing
Forever, again and again.

Trespasser

Blood on her thighs from the long climb
Through waist-high thorns from the sea.
Dust filming the blood, killing
Reflection. Calmly she rolls her palms
In the paste, blunts highlights from her brow.

Dust on the olive as she leans her cheek
Against rough, nightsilvered bark.
Somewhere ahead, a charcoal fire
Spits and hangs heavy on the resiny air
Smoke and fat of a crackling rabbit.

Now she is moving like a gust of night,
Longlegged, slow, upwind of the hunter.
Her lids peel back, knife-slits.
Her eyes dark, flint-shards.
Darts fixed on the point of his neck.

His back to the gully and the moon,
His lungs full of thyme, myrtle,
Smoke of the fire and fat.
He leans back, smug and content,
Lights a last cigarette before turning in.

Kato Zakros

It is called the Gorge of the Dead.
The burial caves are punched in yellow rock,
Spiked by a jewelled fist, an invader's.

Sand underfoot, and dust, everything clear, precise.
Your sandalled foot falls there, and there, and
        there —
The mesmeric clarity of rock and asphodel,

The exact blue of the scarf that binds your hair.
You carry a bent stick as if it were a bow,
And flare at the edges, light coming out of you,

You have the hunter's steady lope, ready to go
Anywhere, risk anything on instinct
And I need water, I need courage, I need rest.

I follow the blue flag and your hair,
Your head a bright bird darting the gorge
Stooping now, and now, and now.

Potsherds, a fragment of rim, a handle-stump —
I stoop to pick them up, sun high between walls
And my head hard in the heat.

I rattle my talismans, hoping to make you turn,
Greasing the potter's thumbprint with my own.
How clear it all is, not a puff of air

Until you punch my lungs with a look.
Hearts leap, I know, I felt it, I still feel it
Here in the dark, tracking you through sunlight.

Voice in an Airport

Out of so many voices, one.
Out of the electric frame,
A single crystal ringing
On and on in empty halls.

For my ear only, as the whole
Departure lounge is for me
Only. Roar at the end of
The runway, four exhausts
Flaming up into the black.

To speak again we will need wire
And fibre optic, satellite ticking
In the blue cold overhead —
Never again a world coiled in a look,
Pulse breathing crystal into pulse.

Corridor Vision, Nuremore Hotel

Behind her eyes
That fugitive thing,
The lock on what is real.

The sweet note, the pain
And what is beyond pain
In a hitch of shoulder, turn
Or tuck of wrist.

She reaches to touch my face and I
Am completely undone.

Walking Shoes

I think of the day we parted and how my heart
    turned,
You were lacing on walking shoes, shoes for your
Winter, shoes for walking away from sunlight,
The room darkening as you straightened &
    looked down.

Later, the cab ticking out towards the airport.
The checking of documents, practical affairs,
And then the tannoy calls to separate terminals,
Panic in look and kiss, departure's business.

You write that yellow leaves are piled in drifts
Near the footbridge where you walk to compose
    yourself.
I imagine them sticking to your shoes, I imagine
    rain,
Walking all day myself against the grain.

Mirror

Silence an ocean, as air is, and we
But small things moving
In a strong light, the last days
Of winter held us fast.

There was a crisp perfection
In the black grass, in the twigs
Laid underfoot, the sweep
Of water coasting the path.

No wind on those days,
Our breath as we walked
trailed streamers in and out
Between the birches.

Each word steps firmly out
And stands in time's mirror.
I set these things down in silence,
Fire for the ice of our old age.

Quiet

What moves hugely in the garden after dark
Is no concern of ours, my love. Be still.

Here we contend with demons of the hearth,
With quiet in our household we may venture out.

You Made your Hair a Sail to Carry Me

Mackerel were turning in slow rolls under the keel,
As we coasted out the wind brought wood- and
    turf-smoke
From bungalows settling for the summer night.
Along the horizon clouds were turning bright.

Away from landfall, away into the west
We bent under sail, the silence of work coming
    over us
As the stars came gleaming out. A wave came on
    abaft
And lifted us, so that the rudder gleamed in air

Before we settled, skipping the shock, into a
    north-running trough.
The long rhythm of it all, the sea, the night, the
    journey,
What your face said when the danger had passed,
And what your hand said tilting my face to the sky,
Is what endures now of the whole year's run.

Eclipse

for PM on her birthday, 25 VI 92

She lifts her skirt above her head
And a black disc hangs in heaven

Her chin is over her shoulder & her eyes
Probe deep into the heft of space.

Silent, and almost without breathing
We watch the spray from her flung hair

Hang shocked and still. Ships crawl on the sea,
Sailors ashore in the loud bars are unsettled.

∞

We light a candle on the windowsill
For a thread of light from here to over there,

Arachne's line, bent silver with her tears,
Child of the zodiac banished into dark.

∞

And slowly our mother lets her skirt fall,
Her wrist leads heavy cloth in a downward arc,

Drawing the black bull forward,
We know that she cannot afford to miss.

Memory packed in his meaty neck,
All that is blood and smoke and pain of pride

In the wide, arrogant sweep of his horns,
The knot of history muscular in his shoulder.

In the steep galleries of shade and fear,
Stars flare as the steel drives home.

∞

I cup Arachne's breast, tilt your bright face
To the moon and me, you kiss me for charm

And promise, your legs float up around my waist
And I jet deep and sure in your womb.

This candleflame gutters in a wind from space,
Tilts left and right, then grips. Downstairs

The sailors are singing and at peace, the air
Is kind, no one at sea tonight will come to harm.

Taverna on the Beach

Pomegranate thumbed open to reveal generations,
Apple split to its white heart of flesh.
Ultramarine waters lap at laughter,
Lacing our days of light with drift of salt.
All night we cry and laugh and you
Taste ash of apple on my skin —
Delighting in apple, pomegranate, light and salt.

Deep in your veins you carry light of salt,
Testing the fruit against dryness under skin.
And unexpected urgencies push through,
Laughter the remedy for the deep fault
Under the streets, the reek of ancient slaughter.
All that the heart and mind can learn from flesh
Piled in a rampart against dead generations.

Watcher

With a head hard since time began
I watch the harvests come and go,
Refusing to choose between the trees and men,
Watching the signatures they make
Spark in the Summer's haze.
I endure this only because I must.

Water draining through the ground beneath me,
Limestone pavement crazed in the sun.
John's Wort sprouts from the fissures,
Blossom and dust straggled in my hair.
The downslope sweating into streams.
Time is the dry leaf of my attention.

Sometimes I see what might be ships from home,
Arcing across the ache, then winking out.
It has been a long station
And still I am unmoved.
At night I stare into the hub of galaxies,
Their wheeling hurts my head.

The Old Man

An old man sits at a crossroads in the dust.
He owns herds and diamonds,
Mines running miles underground,
Cattle numerous as leaves on the dust in autumn.
All day the sun of the world beats on his head.
All day he sits in the light but sees nothing.
Because he is blind, because he is suffocating in
    rage.

He lashes with the sjambok
At anyone who brings him water
At anyone who brings him words
At anyone who says
"Lay down the burden of your cares old man,
We are younger than you and we are many,
We will take up your cares and make them our
    own".

Oh many young men and women say to him
"Lay down the burden of your cares old man
And the light of the world will not be harsh,
The call of the children in their hunger will
    not be sharp,
There will be meat and diamonds, water and milk
For you and your childrens' children and
For us and our childrens' children."

An old man sits at a crossroads in thick dust,
He is blind because he is sitting in his own shadow.

Let him unpick this riddle and we will take him by
    the hand,
When he unpicks this riddle, he will get up
    and walk away.

The High Salt Graveyard

The wind makes pebbles clip
The plastic wreath-case. Pines
Behind me skip and toss,
A dry creaking without cease.

I come to think on his arrested flight,
I come to let the wind blow through me.

The Match Down the Park

for Na Piarsaigh on their fiftieth anniversary

Tom Knott comes bulling out, his shoulder down
bringing weight to bear on the sliothar dropping
From his hand. The crack of ash on leather echoes
The length of the Park.

Like a new evening star, the ball
Climbs the November air, a clean
White flash in the cold and cloud.

All of the faces around me turn
Like plates to the sky, tracking the rising arc.
Over the halfway line now, and dropping into
A clash of hurleys, forward shouldering back.

Our jerseys are brighter than theirs
In this eerie light, the black and amber
Fanning out into a line, a berserk charge.

My face is jammed through the flat bars
Of the gate, the goalposts make me dizzy
Leaning back to look up. Their goalie is jittery,
The chocolate melts in my fist, I hear myself

Howling from a great distance
Come on Piarsaigh, come on, face up, face up . . .
Sound stops in a smell of mud and oranges,

I can feel the weight of them bearing down on goal,
I can't see, Mr. Connery is roaring, and
Johnny Parker,
I bet even my Dad is roaring, back there in the
    crowd
But I can't leave the gate to go see, I can't —

A high ball, a real high one, oh God
Higher than the moon over the fence towards
    Blackrock,
It's dropping in, they're up for it, Pat Kelleher's fist

Closes on leather, knuckles suddenly badged with
    blood
In the overhead clash, he steadies, digs in his heel,
He turns, shoots from the 21 —
The whole field explodes in my face

A goal! A goal! Their keeper stretched across his
    line,
His mouth filled with mud, the sliothar feet from
    my face,
A white bullet bulging the net.

Everything stops.

A ship comes gliding on the high tide, her hull
Floating through the elms over the rust-red stand.
A man on the flying-bridge looks down on us.

I race back to my father, threading the crowd,
Watching for heavy boots, neck twisting back
To the net still bulging, the ship still coming on,
The green flag stabbed aloft, the final whistle.

Sixpence today for the bikeminder under his
    elm.
Men in dark overcoats greeting my Dad
Well done Bert, ye deserved it. And
A great game, haw? Ah dear God what a goal!

I'm introduced as the eldest fella. *Great man
    yourself.*
Men anxious to be home, plucking at bikes,
    pushing away.
The slope to the river, the freighter drawing
    upstream.

And then the long, slow pedal home,
Weaving between the cars on Centre Park Road,
Leaning back into the cradle of his arms.

That was some goal, wasn't it Dad?
It was indeed, it was. His breath warm on my neck,
A wave for the man on Dunlop's gate,
We'll pass the ship tied up near City Hall.

He's a knacky hurler, Pat Kelleher.
    He is Dad, ah jay he is.
By God, that was the way to win.
    It was, Dad, it was.

Skull of a Curlew

Skull of a curlew full of stars,
My mouth on fire with black, unspeakable bees.
Light on the lime boles, bleached and bare,
My gorge rising, crammed with blackfurred bees.

Clay of the orchard on my cheek,
Cheeks puffed like wind on a map's margin.
Dust in each lungful of cold air,
Lips burned on the inside by black bees.

> I wait for the moon to rise me
> I pray to the midnight ant
> I clutch at fistfuls of wet grass
> I hammer the earth with bare heels

Skull of a curlew full of stars,
Night sky dredged with the eyes of bees.
Black fire around each star,
I swallow fear in mouthfuls of fur and wing.

Skull of a curlew full of stars,
The great hive of heaven heavy around me.
I spit out bees and black anger,
Mouth of a curlew, fountain of quiet stars.

From the Sirian Agronomist's Report

So we buried the secret in a grain of sand
And left them to go fork-legged at it,
Inventing plough and husbandry to turn
Their chosen portion of the crust.

Aeons watched mountains fold over over into dust.
Hedged armies manoeuvred and clashed,
Stoop-bellied ships worked out the warp and weft
Until cartographers with their black arts
Trammelled the globe to a version of itself.

In the black book of forgetting
We taught them the war of mind and matter,
In the green of the jungles we laid clue in fly and
    spider,
We stitched their skies with the coded flight of
    birds,
Traced rune and alphabet in crests of the sea.

Water lifted for centuries over their tropics
Draped high aloft the jet-streams, dumped where
    we pleased
And where we did not please in flash-flood, drifts of
    rain,
Tides imperceptible and steep. We tissued their
    lungs,
Made screens for their projections off high crags.

Came a time when their telemetry stabbed crisp
    and stiff
To the far reaches where our ships held
Back and barely out of view.
We thought they had turned the trick inside itself,
By breath and thought and light had found it out.

Still we held off, their jewelled hives winking
A code they neither read nor founded.
The women who knew us we held, counselled and
    caught.
They turned and they turn in our webs and we
    leave them
To go as they please, to speak or to hold their peace.

Sometimes we flash in their skies or we glow in the
    corn.
When the light at evening falls just so on a deserted
        street,
Or a lover is cheered to see death dared in a look,
Redemption in silence — that is us too, and
    more —

As the painter knew, who saw angels on the stairs
When our envoys grew careless or vain,
He caught a formula once in a fragment of
    conversation,
Wrote it down plain. Much good it did them, they
    hear and forget.
Their own worst enemies, our future and our fear.

Rosa Mundi

April, a day off school. Indulged, bored, hungry for
        something new.
The road bends below Driscoll's and I see her
        coming clear,
Laden with shopping bags, eyes bright in the full
        flow of talk.

I've been signalling Collins Barracks on the hill
        across Blackpool,
Morse book open on the window-sill, weighted
        with a cup.
Nobody answering no matter how I flash
        "Help, I am being held prisoner. . ."

It sets in early, disillusion with the State, its idle
        soldiers.
The flash of her eyes as she greets Peg Twomey now.
        I scamper upstairs,
Hook the bevelled mirror back in place. From the
        bedroom window

I see her reach the gate.

∞

How he'd tumble downstairs, crash through the
        front door, taking the
Garden steps two, three at a time. Up close, the
        strain on her face.
Tufnell Park years later, the fireflash of news in my
        face. The silence after.

Grooves in her fingers, released from the heavy
    bags, the rings —
Wedding, engagement, eternity — clicking against
    his nails.
Remembering suddenly when she smiles that he is
    meant to be sick.

Slowly, backwards, up the steps, her scraps of
    thought and talk as she fought
For breath. Who she'd met and who had died, who
    was sick and who had
A new child, news from a world she waded in, hip-
    deep in currents of talk.

A spoon for each of us and a spoon for the pot,
    not forgetting to scald the pot.
What a span of such days unreeling now, my eye on
    them both, reaching
Down through the haze to bring them back, herself
    and her son,

My mother and me.

∞

Dust everywhere when they broke the news, my
    friends, these sudden strangers.
Dust of the Underground on my lips, dust on their
    newpainted window, dust
On the leaves outside, in the heavy air banked high
    over the city.

I stared down at their gate, a vacuum in my chest,
    hands clenching & unclenching.

So easy the words, so treacherous the comfort.
Old enough to know I had failed her,
Too young to know what in, too greedy for life,
    really, to have cared enough.

∞

This is the ring I conjure for them, the stage for
    their dance.
For a child to live, his mother must die. For a man
    to die, his mother must live.
Here on the brink of forty, close to midnight,
    I conjure them all —

My brothers and sisters, my mother and father, my
    neighbours and friends,
The most absolute strangers of my life, my heart's
    companions. Nothing
Is ever lost that has shone light on simple things.

No child is without a mother, no father can lose his
    son,
No mother is unregarded, no sister can fail to learn,
No brother escapes unwounded, no friend can salve
    the burn.

The road bends out into the drunken heft of space
    and nothing can be lost.
Not her life's sacrifice, not our unquenched and
    stubborn love,
Not that child's faith in light flashing from mirrors,
    or her faith in

The human flow of talk. The human flow of talk is
    all we have. Who we've met
And who is sick, who's had a child, who's lost a job.
    Her eyes flash,
He scampers upstairs, rushes downstairs, taking the
    steps two at a time,

Feeding his heart's hunger for life and life only. The
mask of strain on her face,
The ritual of the teapot, hesitant access of heart
    break and knowledge. I would
These words could soothe the pain from her fingers,
    conjure her patient grace.